IRISH COTTAGES

An Irish cottage is made from the land, built by the people, for the people, and because of these reasons, its existance could never clash with the landscape.

I hope that, what the reader will become aware of, when he or she looks through this book is a story about Ireland, told almost without words.

Joe Reynolds

GW00706183

♥ *Little Books*
of Ireland

First published by
REAL IRELAND DESIGN LIMITED
27 Beechwood Close, Boghall Rd., Bray, Co. Wicklow, Ireland.
Tel: (01) 2860799, 2867545, 2867844. Fax: (01) 2829962.
1989 1990 1992 1996

IRISH COTTAGES
ISBN 0 946887 25 X

COTTAGE
BALLYVAUGHAN, CO. CLARE.

COTTAGE WINDOW
BUNRATTY FOLK PARK, CO. CLARE.

THATCHED COTTAGE
BALLYCONNEELY, CO. GALWAY.

DERELICT COTTAGE

TWO STOREY COTTAGE
GLENCOLUMKILLE, CO. DONEGAL.

THATCHED COTTAGE
BLOODY FORELAND, CO. DONEGAL.

OUTBUILDINGS
CO. DONEGAL.

THATCHED COTTAGE
KILCOLGAN, CO. GALWAY.

THATCHED COTTAGE.

TIN ROOFED COTTAGE
TRIM, CO. MEATH.

COTTAGE WINDOW
WEXFORD TOWN.

THATCHED COTTAGE
CARNA, CO. GALWAY.

THATCHED COTTAGE
CROHY HEAD, CO. DONEGAL.

COTTAGE
GLENESH VALLEY, CO. DONEGAL.

THATCHED COTTAGE
ADARE, CO. LIMERICK

THATCHED COTTAGE
GLENCOLUMBKILLE, CO. DONEGAL.

COTTAGE
ARTHURSTOWN, CO. WEXFORD.

THATCHED COTTAGE
PORTMARNOCK, CO. DUBLIN.

COTTAGE
CROAGH PATRICK, CO. MAYO.

THATCHED COTTAGE
ROUNDSTONE, CO. GALWAY.

OUTBUILDINGS
NORTH DONEGAL.

THATCHED COTTAGE
KINVARA, CO. GALWAY.

COTTAGE
WATERFORD TOWN.

TWO STOREY COTTAGE
WEST CORK.

TWO STOREY COTTAGE
ALLIHIES, CO. CORK.

COTTAGE
SLIEVE BLOOM MOUNTAINS, CO. LAOIS.

GATE LODGE
WICKLOW TOWN.

TWO STOREY COTTAGE
RING OF KERRY.

COTTAGE
MILLTOWN MALBAY, CO. CLARE.

COTTAGE DOOR
CROHY HEAD, CO. DONEGAL.